T0016598

MAXIMIZED
MINUTES
FOR
FATHERS

Edwin Louis Cole

MAXIMIZED
MINUTES
FOR
FATHERS

WHITAKER
HOUSE

Maximized Minutes for Fathers

Christian Men's Network • P.O. Box 3 • Grapevine, TX 76099
ChristianMensNetwork.com
facebook.com/edwinlouiscole/
facebook.com/ChristianMensNetwork/

ISBN: 978-1-64123-852-6
Printed in the United States of America
© 2016, 2022 by Edwin and Nancy Cole Legacy LLC

Whitaker House • 1030 Hunt Valley Circle • New Kensington, PA 15068
www.whitakerhouse.com

Library of Congress Control Number: 2022934674

1 2 3 4 5 6 7 8 9 10 11 ⨆ 29 28 27 26 25 24 23 22

CONTENTS

CREATING YOUR
HOME ENVIRONMENT

A father's responsibility is to provide intimacy, discipline, love, and value for his family. Gangs and cults are counterfeit families, because they provide all four. Family life gives personal fulfillment to the individual. God created the family for that purpose. People are social creatures and need fulfillment. The home and church are the places God intends for us to find the greatest sense of fulfillment.

Choose you this day whom [you] will serve...but as for me and my house, we will serve the Lord.   Joshua 24:15 KJV

Unless the Lord builds the house, they labor in vain who build it.

Psalm 127:1 NKJV

FAMILY MEANS
"FATHER'S HOUSE."

Virtue is worth fighting for. National cemeteries are full of heroic loved ones who died fighting for the virtue of freedom. Women have died defending their virtue. Fathers have died protecting their children's virtue.

Loyalty is a virtue of the faithful. Gentleness is a virtue of the strong. Freedom is a virtue of a nation. Courage is the virtue of the wise.

Never tire of loyalty and kindness. Hold these virtues tightly. Write them deep within your heart.   Proverbs 3:3 TLB

MEN, FAMILIES, AND NATIONS ARE NOT GREAT BY THE VIRTUE OF THEIR WEALTH BUT BY THE WEALTH OF THEIR VIRTUE.

Harmony is comprised of sounds played in respect, one for another, by people in an orchestra who are respectful of one another. Musicians play in respect of one another, in respect of time.

Musicians use respect and time to make a symphony. Families use respect and time to make harmony.

Harmony is as refreshing as the dew...on the mountains.   Psalm 133:3 TLB

Search for peace, and work to maintain it.   Psalm 34:14 NLT

Better is a dry morsel with quietness, than a house full of feasting with strife.
                              Proverbs 17:1 NKJV

HARMONY IN THE HOME IS A SWEET SOUND.

It's time for each of us to accept the responsibility God created for us to exercise, including that of being strong fathers. Providing a solution to fatherlessness is society's only hope!

Now that I am old and gray, do not abandon me, O God. Let me proclaim your power to this new generation, your mighty miracles to all who come after me.   Psalm 71:18 NLT

ELDERS MUST TEACH YOUNGER MEN. WE CANNOT LET OUR WISDOM DIE WITH US.

Television and the Internet are like a thief. A thief steals time, kills initiative, destroys relationships.

The thief comes only to steal and kill and destroy; I have come that they may have life, and have it to the full.

John 10:10 NIV

Through laziness, the rafters sag; because of idle hands, the house leaks.

Ecclesiastes 10:18 NIV

GIVING YOUR FAMILY YOUR TIME SHOWS RESPECT FOR THEM.

God reveals himself as our Father. We reveal ourselves as father to those we have birthed. The priest in the Old Testament was intercessor between God and man, the mediator, the one who ministered God's grace to the people in his care. In the same way, the father in the home acts as "priest," praying for the family and administering God's grace to them.

Do not be anxious about anything, but in every situation, by prayer and petition, with thanksgiving, present your requests to God.   Philippians 4:6 NIV

NO MAN HAS THE RIGHT TO TALK TO HIS CHILDREN ABOUT GOD UNTIL HE FIRST TALKS TO GOD ABOUT HIS CHILDREN.

Intimacy in spirit is more than in word and brings bonding in relationship. Prayer knows no distance.

Reverence for God gives a man deep strength; his children have a place of refuge and security.   Proverbs 14:26 TLB

They joined with the other believers in regular attendance at...prayer meetings... And shared everything with each other.
Acts 2:42-44 TLB

PRAYER PRODUCES INTIMACY. YOU BECOME INTIMATE WITH THE ONE FOR WHOM YOU PRAY, WITH WHOM YOU PRAY AND TO WHOM YOU PRAY.

FATHER AS LEADER

Fathers provide the family's value system. They provide the atmosphere in the home, whether present or absent. Children learn theory at school, but how to live at home.

Train up a child in the way he should go: and when he is old, he will not depart from it.   Proverbs 22:6 KJV

HOME IS THE SCHOOL OF FIRST INSTRUCTION.

Every child sees his or her father as a hero. Drug dealers and predators know your child's need of a hero. God placed a desire in every man's heart to be successful, to be a hero and a champion. Every father can be a hero to his family. Heroes are simply men who act in a moment of time on a need greater than self.

Children's children *are* the crown of old men, and the glory of children *are* their fathers.   Proverbs 17:6 KJV

MEN DREAM OF THEMSELVES AS HEROES. WOMEN DREAM OF MEN AS HEROES. CHILDREN *SEE* MEN AS HEROES.

Canceling family plans is giving priority to something other than the family. Children don't understand it. Children accept it, but it will never be erased from their minds or emotions. Avoid family crisis by keeping your word and carrying out your plans. Your word is your bond. You make covenant when you give your word. Not to perform it breaks covenant with those to whom it is given.

My heart is set on fulfilling your statutes; they are my reward forever.

Psalm 119:112 NABRE

KEEPING YOUR WORD PRODUCES INFLUENCE FOR THE KINGDOM OF GOD.

Fathers too often reduce fathering to paying the bills, providing a home and education, allowing recreation, administering an occasional lecture, and, at various times and in varying degrees, being the disciplinarian.

But fathering is a comprehensive task. It means thinking, studying, monitoring, recommending, influencing, and loving.

Whatever you do or say, let it be as a representative of the Lord Jesus.

Colossians 3:17 TLB

FOLLOWERS "HAPPEN" TO INFLUENCE BUT LEADERS "DETERMINE" TO INFLUENCE.

Young people learn to have good interpersonal relationships from their encounters at homes. The dinner hour is one of the most important hours in a child's life. It is a time for learning to communicate. Many fathers lose this valuable opportunity to be with their family. It is a tragedy when, instead of utilizing the dinner hour to establish relationships and strengthen ties in the family, it is squandered. The dinner hour is the hour that is made for listening, as well as sharing the hurts, pains, victories, and blessings of the day.

Teach [God's Words] to your children. Talk about them when you are at home and when you are on the road, when you are going to bed and when you are getting up...so that as long as the sky remains above the earth, you and your children may flourish.

Deuteronomy 11:19, 21 NLT

EVERYTHING IN LIFE IS BASED ON RELATIONSHIPS.

To be a good father, you must first learn to be a good son. If you haven't had a good father helping to bring you through the process of maturation into the maturity of manhood, you'll have difficulty in becoming a good father yourself. Because my dad wasn't a good father, I lacked qualities of real fatherhood in raising my own children. But, through a relationship with God through Jesus Christ, his grace compensated for my lack. Through Jesus Christ, we are adopted into the family of God and, as good sons of God, are taught to be good earthly fathers.

For I know him [Abraham], that he will command his [children] and his household after him, and they shall keep the way of the Lord.   Genesis 18:19 KJV

TO THE DEGREE THAT YOU BECOME A GOOD SON TO GOD, YOU BECOME A GOOD FATHER TO YOUR CHILDREN.

To accept responsibility, make wise decisions, and serve those he loves are three marks of a man. Irresponsibility, foolishness, and insensitivity are blemishes on his character. Decisions determine conduct, character, and destiny. Everything in life is under our power of choice, but once we make the choice, we become the servant to it. Life is composed of our choices and constructed by our words. When we let others make our choices for us, or tell us who and what we are, we let them create our world.

The pattern for demise is: Deception — Denial — Distraction — Dislocation — Disruption — Destruction

The pattern for profit is: Decision — Dedication — Discipline — Detail

Everything is permissible for me, but not all things are beneficial. Everything is permissible for me, but I will not be enslaved by anything [and brought under its power, allowing it to control me].

1 Corinthians 6:12 AMP

THE FATHER'S RESPONSIBILITY IS NOT TO MAKE ALL THE CHILD'S DECISIONS, BUT TO LET THE CHILD OBSERVE THE FATHER MAKING HIS.

For generations, men were taught to bring their families to church and the church will take the responsibility to disciple the family through Sunday school, youth programs, Bible studies, and other activities. In so doing, the pastor becomes the surrogate father to every member of every family. That is a burden too heavy for any one man to bear.

The greatest value of a father's legacy is in the faith he leaves in his child's life. His child's greatest treasure is his faith in God. It is of such value, in fact, that it is invaluable.

All who fear God and trust in him are blessed beyond expression. Yes, happy is the man who delights in doing his commands. His children shall be honored everywhere, for good men's sons have a special heritage.   Psalm 112:1-2 TLB

When your children ask in time to come, saying, "What do these stones *mean* to you?" Then you shall answer them.

Joshua 4:6-7 NKJV

GOD'S PATTERN TO DISCIPLE THE FAMILY IS: THE PASTOR DISCIPLES THE MAN, THE MAN DISCIPLES THE FAMILY.

Serving produces greatness. General Motors Corporation became one of the world's greatest companies because it served so many people. Serving produces greatness. Serving the family makes the father great.

———

Anyone who takes care of a little child like this is caring for me! And whoever cares for me is caring for God who sent me. Your care for others is the measure of your greatness.   Luke 9:48 TLB

YOUR CARE FOR OTHERS IS THE MEASURE OF YOUR GREATNESS.

Leaders can never stop serving, for when they do, they will no longer be qualified to lead. Serving is ministry. Learning to minister, serve capably and well, work for the benefit of others, is the quality that makes a leader. Even Christ took a towel and washed His disciples' feet.

Everything we do in life is service — Washing dishes, making the bed, mowing the lawn, washing the car, designing computer software, milking the cow, selling a car — all is based on service. Whatever we do in serving others we are to do as unto the Lord, which calls for our best effort.

Whoever wants to be great must become a servant... That is what the Son of Man has done: He came to serve, not to be served.   Mark 10:44-45 MSG

Whatever you do, do it all for the glory of God.   1 Corinthians 10:31 NIV

LEADERS ARE QUALIFIED TO LEAD TO THE DEGREE THEY ARE WILLING TO SERVE.

A FATHER'S LOVE

Many men would rather give their wives the checkbook than a warm embrace or loving kiss. Why? It's simply easier to give money than oneself. Many men would rather buy their children things than spend time with them. It's easier. But, giving of self is evidence of love.

You cannot compensate by sacrifice what you lose through disobedience. Nothing, no gift, can substitute for the love of a father.

Obedience is far better than sacrifice.
1 Samuel 15:22 TLB

Greater love has no one than this: to lay down one's life for one's friends.
John 15:13 NIV

GIVING CANNOT COMPENSATE FOR A LACK OF LOVE.

A childish man is an immature man. When a man acts like a child, he forces his wife to act like his mother. Fatherlessness is caused by the immaturity of men. It is a pandemic problem in every nation on the planet.

You are only young once, but you can live immature for a lifetime. Maturity doesn't come with age but begins with the acceptance of responsibility.

At one end of the spectrum, some men can't accept responsibility for their own actions, and at the other end are men who not only accept responsibility for themselves but also for their relationships and their family. Every man has the option as to which he will be.

Husbands, love your wives and do not become bitter against them.

Ephesians 5:25 NASB

THE GREATEST THING A FATHER CAN DO FOR HIS CHILDREN IS TO LOVE THEIR MOTHER.

Two people can share the same name and live under the same roof and be miles apart in spirit. A man may go to church, sing the songs, and read the Bible and be miles from God because there is no love for him in the heart. Love is the quality that brings intimacy to life. The love of a father is the quality that brings intimacy with his children.

As cold waters to a thirsty soul, so is good news from a far country.

Proverbs 25:25 KJV

Better is a neighbor that is near than a brother far off.   Proverbs 27:10 KJV

DISTANCE IS NOT ONLY MEASURED BY MILES, BUT BY AFFECTION.

God can command us to love because love centers in the will, not the emotions. Turn your heart toward love. Rid yourself of every other motivation. Allow the love of God to motivate you in your fatherhood.

I will love thee, O Lord, my strength.
Psalm 18:1 KJV

I demand that you love each other as much as I love you.   John 15:12 TLB

LOVE CENTERS IN THE WILL. THEREFORE, IT CAN BE COMMANDED.

There is faith, hope, and love, but "the greatest of these is love" is the order the Bible gives us. The reason that love is greater is because love has no end. Faith and hope will end when what faith has obtained and hope has realized comes. Love will continue on. Love is eternal because God is love. To love as God loves, his love must be in the heart of a man.

The greatest of these is love…
1 Corinthians 13:13 TLB

LOVE IS THE ONLY THING THAT WILL NEVER FAIL — THAT'S WHY IT'S "THE GREATEST."

God is a good God. He is at work in you to produce your highest good. God has a plan for your success. To walk in God's will for our lives, as real men, secure in our manhood and our relationship with Him, is our highest good. Our highest good gives God pleasure. When we please God, we are working for our own highest good.

We can trust the will of God, because God always wills and works toward our highest good. Likewise, your children trust your leadership when you are always working toward their highest good.

And we know that God causes everything to work together for the good of those who love God and are called according to his purpose for them.   Romans 8:28 NLT

"For I know the plans I have for you," declares the LORD, "plans to prosper you and not to harm you, plans to give you hope and a future."   Jeremiah 29:11 NIV

TO LOVE SOMEONE IS TO WORK FOR THEIR HIGHEST GOOD.

Speaking the truth in love is the manner and spirit of telling the truth. Love is the qualification for speaking the truth, both in teaching and in family relationships. The spirit in which truth is spoken determines whether or not it is received. Affection guarantees reception.

Fathers, provoke not your children to anger, lest they be discouraged.

Colossians 3:21 KJV

But speaking the truth in love, [in all things—both our speech and our lives expressing His truth], let us grow up in all things. Ephesians 4:15 AMP

LOVE IS THE QUALIFICATION FOR SPEAKING THE TRUTH.

The evidence and provisions of love are those in God's own nature that are required in fathers. Husbands are to love wives as Christ loves the Church. The evidences of love are selflessness, the desire to benefit the one loved, and a desire for unity. Likewise, fathers love their children and provide for them what God provides. The provisions of love are identity, security, and stability.

Whoever has my commands and keeps them is the one who loves me. The one who loves me will be loved by my Father, and I too will love them and show myself to them.   John 14:21 NIV

THE WAY WE LOVE OTHERS AND OUR RELATIONSHIP TO THEM IS THE EVIDENCE OF OUR LOVE FOR GOD AND OUR RELATIONSHIP TO HIM.

We know how much God loves us by how much he gave for us. Christ proved his love by giving himself for us. In marriage, husbands and wives know how much each loves the other—by how much of themselves they give to each other. The difference between deadly dads and fabulous fathers is known by the degree they give themselves to their family. Gestures communicate. The gesture of giving confirms loving words.

For God so loved the world, that he gave his only begotten Son, that whosoever believeth in him should not perish, but have everlasting life.   John 3:16 KJV

YOU KNOW THE DEPTH OF LOVING BY THE DEGREE OF GIVING.

There is nothing weak or wimpy about saying, "I LOVE YOU." Those words need to be said— to God, to your children—again and again. Men who are truly men are not ashamed of the reality of true love, neither are they embarrassed to admit love or to express it. They show it in word, gesture, and spirit.

Fathers who try to satisfy their children with impersonal gifts rather than through a personal loving relationship will always have trouble. Nothing impersonal can ever substitute for personal love.

I want you to be leaders also in the spirit of cheerful giving.... This is one way to prove that your love is real, that it goes beyond mere words.

2 Corinthians 8:7-8 TLB.

THE TRUE ROOT OF GIVING IS ALWAYS BASED ON LOVING.

The nature of love is found in the quality of giving. That is evidenced by God the Father giving his only begotten Son for our salvation and also by the man who knows how to be a real father by exploring the love of God.

Let's not merely say that we love each other; let us show the truth by our actions.   John 3:18 NLT

YOU CAN GIVE WITHOUT LOVING, BUT YOU CANNOT LOVE WITHOUT GIVING.

A FATHER'S
COMMUNICATION

Communication is the basis for life. When communication stops, abnormality sets in. The ultimate end of abnormality is death. God created man to live normally—in fellowship with him. Sin brought the abnormality of separation. Death was the result. That process is in all of life, including human relationships.

With the "prodigal son," when the prodigal broke off communication with his father and separated himself, he began to live an abnormal life. Only when he came to himself and repented was he able to restore communication, which led to reconciliation and restoration.

If you do not remain in me, you are like a branch that is thrown away and withers; such branches are picked up, thrown into the fire and burned.   John 15:6 NIV

Teach them to your children, talking about them when you sit at home and when you walk along the road, when you lie down and when you get up.

Deuteronomy 11:19 NIV

WHEN COMMUNICATION STOPS, ABNORMALITY SETS IN. IF YOU DON'T COMMUNICATE, YOU CAN'T RELATE.

The art of communication is not based on speaking but on listening. A great father is a good listener. Listening has the power of healing.

A man cannot hear the needs of his family when he is listening to the demands of a monitor or screen. Nor can his family learn healthy communication through casual exchanges sitting beside an impersonal box.

When dad starts listening, lost family members are rediscovered right in the home, old loves are rekindled, fathers are reunited emotionally with their children, relationships are reestablished, children learn to interact with adults once again.

This is the confidence we have in approaching God: that if we ask anything according to his will, he hears us.

1 John 5:14 NIV

The more words you speak, the less they mean.　　　Ecclesiastes 6:11 TLB

THE ART OF COMMUNICATION IS BASED ON LISTENING.

Young men and women admire and emulate athletes who have fame as a result of their ability. For athletes to refuse to accept responsibility as a role model for the young is simply disregarding societal duty. In the same way, fathers who tell their children, "Don't do as I do, do as I say," are absolving themselves of responsibility to set a pattern of behavior for their children to imitate.

The apostle Paul willingly accepted the responsibility of being a role model for every believer in his day, saying, "Follow my example, as I follow the example of Christ." We still do.

Follow my example, as I follow the example of Christ.   1 Corinthians 11:1 NIV

Don't lord it over the people assigned to your care, but lead them by your own good example.   1 Peter 5:3 NLT

CHILDREN MAY NOT ALWAYS LISTEN TO YOU, BUT THEY WILL ALWAYS IMITATE YOU.

Listening is as important as loving. Listening is the basic art of communication. You don't make a success in life by your ability to speak but by your ability to listen. The art is shown in leadership, counseling, salesmanship, marriage, and fatherhood.

Wherefore, my beloved brethren, let every man be swift to hear, slow to speak, slow to wrath.   James 1:19 KJV

LISTENING IS A VIRTUE OF LOVING.

Taking time to listen shows respect for others. But not everything people say deserves to be heard. Listening to foolish people shows disrespect for self.

Spouting off before listening to the facts is both shameful and foolish.

Proverbs 18:13 NLT

Even fools are thought wise if they keep silent, and discerning if they hold their tongues.

Proverbs 17:28 NIV

THE MAN WHO LISTENS BEFORE HE TALKS IS WISE.

The common man stops the habit of study or reading after his schooling, but the uncommon man continues to read and study all through life. Reading keeps him from aging as others do. Keeping the mind active is an agent against aging. Reading is the most inexpensive thing a man can do, and not doing it the most expensive.

Give attention to reading.

1 Timothy 4:13 NKJV

How sweet are your words to my taste, sweeter than honey to my mouth! I gain understanding from your precepts; therefore I hate every wrong path. Your word is a lamp for my feet, a light on my path.

Psalm 119:103-105 NIV

READING IS AN ART FORM, AND EVERY MAN CAN BE AN ARTIST.

Reading is the one ingredient in child development that bonds parent and child closest and easiest. The loss of the love of reading, habit of reading, and pursuit of reading is the gain in the realm of ignorance. Reading develops the power of concentration, so you can understand what is read. Learning to read is one of the four "R's" — reading, writing, arithmetic and religion.

Place these words on your hearts. Get them deep inside you. Tie them on your hands and foreheads as a reminder. Teach them to your children.

Deuteronomy 11:20 MSG

I have taught you in the way of wisdom; I have led you in right paths. When you walk, your steps will not be hindered, And when you run, you will not stumble.

Proverbs 4:11-12 NKJV

THE GREATEST SIGHT IN ALL THE WORLD IS THE SIGHT OF A DAD READING THE BIBLE TO HIS CHILDREN.

The power of choice is our only true freedom in life, but once we make the choice, we become the servant to it. To change our life, we must change the choices we make and the words we use.

Words are power, and life and death are in the power of the tongue. We live on the basis of the words others have spoken to us that we have received into our life or the words we have spoken which have become the basis of our belief and conduct.

Death and life are in the power of the tongue.   Proverbs 18:21 KJV

WORDS HAVE CREATIVE POWER.

God's Word is his bond. It is the expression of his nature and the measure of his character. God's Word is magnified above his name. We believe in God's name because we believe his Word. God's Word is the sole source of faith and the absolute rule of conduct.

We are made in the image of God. God gave us creative power with our words. Our word is to be our bond. Our word is the expression of our nature and the measure of our character. Our word is magnified above our name. People believe our "name" or reputation, because they believe our words. Our word is the source of faith and rule of conduct for those to whom we give it.

Do not swear, either by heaven or by earth or with any other oath. But let your "Yes" be "Yes," and *your* "No," "No."

James 5:12 NKJV

AS GOD'S WORD IS TO US, OUR WORD IS TO BE TO OTHERS.

Don't sacrifice your family on the altar of your business or ministry or hobby. Your family comes first, and must not be given the dregs of what you didn't give to others. Because they have committed their lives to you, and their lives depend on you, they must be respected by taking first place in your life. Too many men set their business calendar, then find they don't have time to do what the family wants, or find that the family cannot do what they want. This makes the family feel like second-class citizens. Set your family calendar first. Give your family preeminence.

A good man out of the good treasure of his heart brings forth good; and an evil man out of the evil treasure of his heart brings forth evil. For out of the abundance of the heart his mouth speaks.

Luke 6:45 NKJV

And I tell you this, you must give an account on judgment day for every idle word you speak.   Matthew 12:36 NLT

A BROKEN PROMISE, TO A CHILD, IS THE SAME AS A LIE.

BUILDING YOUR
CHILD'S CHARACTER

The character of the leader is shown in the characteristics of his family, company, or church. Where change is necessary, it must come voluntarily from the top, or it will come involuntarily from the bottom. Revelation is always better than revolution.

When good people run things, everyone is glad, but when the ruler is bad, everyone groans.　　　　Proverbs 29:2 MSG

THE CHARACTERISTICS OF THE KINGDOM EMANATE FROM THE CHARACTER OF THE KING.

Street-wise kids are profane, hard of heart, manipulative, deceptive in spirit, and insolent in manner. They con parents, and do things only to impress. Church-wise kids are profane, hard of heart, manipulative, deceptive in spirit, and insolent in manner. They con parents, and do things only to impress. They are really just con artists. The only real difference between them is that one is religious while the other is profane.

God looks on the heart, not the façade. If your child is in that kind of church-wise group, get them away. It takes courage to resist the peer pressure of friends – courage not to go with the crowd. Help your children add courage to their faith.

Be not wise in your own conceits.
Romans 12:16 KJV

They will go to church, yes, but they won't really believe anything they hear. Don't be taken in by people like that.
2 Timothy 3:5 TLB

BUILDING YOUR CHILD'S CHARACTER

THE CHURCH-WISE ARE LIKE THE STREET-WISE BUT ARE NOT GOD-WISE.

You imbibe the spirit of those to whom you open your heart and become like them. Choose carefully. Open your heart to those whose spirit is holy, pure, sweet, good, and acceptable.

Be not deceived: evil communications corrupt good manners.

1 Corinthians 15:33 KJV

OPEN THE HEART, IMBIBE THE SPIRIT.

Failing is not the worst thing in the world — quitting is. Failure is the womb of success. Success is born out of failure. Better to try to do something and fail, than to quit and succeed in doing nothing. Champions practice in private to succeed in public. Success swallows failure. Encourage your child.

Be on the alert, stand firm in the faith, act like men, be strong.

1 Corinthians 16:13 NASB

CHAMPIONS ARE NOT THOSE WHO NEVER FAIL, BUT THOSE WHO NEVER QUIT.

The practice of reading develops the power of concentration, encourages creative thinking, broadens understanding, increases sharpness of mind and enjoyment of life. Television, audios, and videos through electronics are all great technological marvels, but they usurp the skill of reading. In 1644, Massachusetts passed a law making fathers responsible for teaching children to read. Listening is the first thing you learn in life, speaking is next, reading is third. In your child's maturity, reading is still the most important.

How can a young person live a clean life? By carefully reading the map of your Word.   Psalm 119:9 MSG

LISTENING COMES FIRST IN LIFE, BUT IN MATURITY, IT COMES AFTER READING.

Without a good foundation, any building will collapse. The structure doesn't uphold the building, the foundation does. Foundations are dug before anything else can be built. Building a foundation for life involves: Discipline to study. Overcoming the temptations to play. Standing strong in the rigors of daily devotion. Teaching your children to know when to be tough.

It is good for people to submit at an early age to the yoke of his discipline.

Lamentations 3:27 NLT

THE MORE YOU DISCIPLINE EARLY IN LIFE THE EASIER IT WILL BE LATER IN LIFE.

Truth is not an option in life. The more you base your life on truth, the better will be your way, and the greater will be your life. Truth eliminates guilt, fear, and hiding. The truth alone can set you free. Truth is without partiality. Truth can never die. Truth will stand the test of time.

Jesus said to him, "I am the way, and the truth, and the life."   John 14:6 NASB

THE KINGDOM OF GOD RUNS ON TRUTH, NOT SENTIMENT.

To trust what is either short of or beyond truth is to trust in a lie. To promise, or give people your word, and not keep it is to teach them not to trust you. True of employees, vendors, citizens, wives, and true of your children.

The righteous *man* walks in his integrity;
His children *are* blessed after him.
                                    Proverbs 20:7 NKJV

TRUST IS EXTENDED TO THE LIMIT OF TRUTH AND NO MORE.

Love truth. You may know truth, recognize it, admit it, but not love it. To love truth is to make it a part of your life. Truth, honesty, faith, love, humility, wisdom, courage—all are virtues of manhood a father teaches his children.

Then you will know the truth, and the truth will set you free.   John 8:32 NIV

THE MORE YOU BASE
YOUR LIFE ON TRUTH,
THE BETTER WILL BE
YOUR WAY AND THE
GREATER WILL BE
YOUR LIFE.

Trust, and even more trust, are both given. To lie, be unfaithful and deceive, is to be untrustworthy. All untrustworthiness is the result of character defects.

He shall cover you with His feathers, and under His wings you shall take refuge; His truth shall be your shield and buckler. Psalms 91:4 NKJV

THE REWARD OF THE TRUSTWORTHY IS MORE TRUST.

You are never too young to hear from God. Daniel was taken captive in his teens and recorded his final vision over sixty years later. His life proves beyond doubt you're never too young and never too old to hear from the Lord.

You are never too old, and never too young to learn. You're never too young to be taught and never too old to teach. You are never too old…and you're never too young.

───────────────

My sheep hear my voice, and I know them, and they follow me.

John 10:27 KJV

"O Lord God," I said, "I can't do that! I'm far too young! I'm only a youth!" "Don't say that," he replied, "for you will go wherever I send you and speak whatever I tell you to. And don't be afraid of the people, for I, the Lord, will be with you and see you through." Jeremiah 1:6-8 TLB

HEARING FROM GOD DOESN'T DEPEND ON AGE BUT ON RELATIONSHIP.

GUIDING YOUR
CHILD'S MATURITY

Accountability is a requirement for responsibility. Authority is given only to those who can accept responsibility. To give authority without accountability is to allow anarchy. It is like giving a match to an arsonist.

Responsibility is a basic characteristic of maturity. Teach your children to be responsible for decisions they make. Then hold them accountable for their decisions and actions.

For everyone to whom much is given; from him much will be required.

Luke 12:48 NKJV

NEVER GIVE AUTHORITY WITHOUT ACCOUNTABILITY.

Lines drawn on the street are not the highway department trying to keep people from having fun driving, but to keep motorists from killing themselves. So parents draw lines of behavior, not to keep children from having a good time, but to keep them from danger and harm. Remove barriers and restraint to aberrations and aberration soon appears normal. God's boundaries are for our pleasure to give us life more abundantly.

Oh, how I love your instructions! I think about them all day long. Your word is a lamp to guide my feet and a light for my path.   Psalm 119:97, 105 NLT

BOUNDARIES ARE TO PROTECT LIFE, NOT TO LIMIT PLEASURES.

Recognize that your children were created by God to be successful, to be heroes and champions. Recognize their gifts, talents, and abilities and help them dedicate those abilities to God.

Scripture teaches that God is the author and finisher of our faith. If God implants his desires in our hearts, then he will see to it that they are completed as we submit to his Lordship and work in cooperation with his Spirit within us. That is how his kingdom is able to come to earth through us.

Delight yourself also in the LORD, and He shall give you the desires of your heart. Commit your way to the LORD, trust also in Him, and He shall bring *it* to pass.
Psalm 37:4-5 NKJV

GOD AUTHORS DESIRES IN YOUR HEART, THEN FULFILLS HIS WILL BY ENABLING YOU TO REALIZE THOSE DESIRES.

It is your spiritual DNA that determines the spirit of your home, and it is your guidance that determines the atmosphere of the home. What you allow or what you disallow in your home becomes the atmosphere of your home. Build an expectation of what is right or wrong—items allowed in a child's room, the media allowed in your car, the music you play in your private time—it's all up to you. Then follow the same maxim at home as at work: to have "expect" you must follow with "inspect."

Because the sentence against an evil deed is not executed quickly, therefore the hearts of the sons of men among them are given fully to do evil.

Ecclesiastes 8:11 NASB

PEOPLE DO WHAT YOU INSPECT, NOT WHAT YOU EXPECT.

It's not what is said, but what is done. Change is not change until it is change. You can think about change, intend to do it, imagine it is done, talk about it, but it is not done until it is done. People are not paid for what they intend to do, but for what they do. Children are not rewarded for what they intended to do, but for what they did.

———

Search me, O God, and know my heart; test my thoughts. Point out anything in me that offends you, and lead me along the path of everlasting life.

Psalm 139:23, 24 TLB/NLT

You, then, why do you judge your brother or sister? Or why do you treat them with contempt? For we will all stand before God's judgment seat.

Romans 14:10 NIV

MOST PEOPLE JUDGE OTHERS BY THEIR ACTIONS AND THEMSELVES BY THEIR INTENTIONS.

God says, "He that hath an ear let him hear." Hearing is necessary to doing. Doing without hearing is folly.

———————————————

I, Wisdom, give good advice and common sense. Because of my strength, kings reign in power, and rulers make just laws. I love all who love me. Those who search for me shall surely find me.

Proverbs 8:14-17 TLB

LEARNING BY LISTENING IS BETTER THAN LEARNING BY MISTAKES.

Indolence and insolence are often the characteristics of the undisciplined. Indolence is doing nothing, and insolence is passing blame on to others. Some children turn off to education because they never learned how to learn. The lazy try to cover their failures with excuses, but they are not acceptable. Excuses are not reasons.

Laziness and ignorance go hand in hand. "The lazy man is brother to the saboteur," the Bible says. Laziness sabotages a child's future.

And do not be conformed to this world, but be transformed by the renewing of your mind, that you may prove what *is* that good and acceptable and perfect will of God.   Romans 12:2 NKJV

AN IDLE MIND IS THE PLAYGROUND OF THE DEVIL.

CORRECTING YOUR
CHILD'S BEHAVIOR

The popular notion is that maturity comes with age. Not true. You get old with age. Maturing comes by the acceptance of responsibility. Accepting responsibility for our failures is the substance on which success rests. No one can be responsible for success unless he is willing to accept responsibility for failure.

Not that I have already obtained all this, or have already arrived at my goal, but I press on to take hold of that for which Christ Jesus took hold of me.

Philippians 3:12 NIV

YOU ARE ONLY QUALIFIED TO BE RESPONSIBLE FOR SUCCESS TO THE DEGREE YOU ARE WILLING TO BE RESPONSIBLE FOR FAILURE.

We cannot bear the sins of others. Forgiveness is God's way to set us free from others' sins. Unforgiveness closes. Forgiveness opens. Unforgiveness binds. Forgiveness releases. If you forgive, you release. By not forgiving you retain.

Your forgiveness of others is your greatest gift to them. When God forgives us, he remembers our sins against us no more.

Receive the Holy Spirit. If you forgive anyone's sins, they are forgiven. If you do not forgive them, they are not forgiven.

John 20:22-23 NLT

IF YOU FORGIVE, YOU RELEASE; IF YOU DO NOT FORGIVE, YOU RETAIN.

One of the most subtle catastrophes of past decades has been the "antihero" syndrome that has almost eliminated positive heroes and left us bereft of role models as patriotic examples. The hero image in the minds of young children powerfully motivates them in life. The distance between the ideal and the real is the degree of disappointment in life. But children need the ideal. Children need heroes that can affect them for good. How can we change the negative, antihero images? By working to renew the images in our children's minds.

Be renewed in the spirit of your mind.
Ephesians 4:23 NKJV

IF YOU CAN CHANGE AN IMAGE, YOU CAN CHANGE A BEHAVIOR.

God never begins or ends on a negative. God's plan for us begins with the positive and will end with the positive. In God's pattern for our lives, we grow, expand, enlarge, and accept greater responsibility to reach maturity. If we fail a test of growth, he brings us back ready to pass the test, to replace failure with success.

When dealing with your children, start with a positive and end with a positive.

I am certain that God, who began the good work within you, will continue his work until it is finally finished.

Philippians 1:6 NLT

GOD NEVER ENDS ANYTHING ON A NEGATIVE. GOD ALWAYS ENDS ON A POSITIVE.

Children need to feel loved and valued. With children, the reward must balance the punishment, the caress must balance the correction. Discipline requires toughness. But we need both the tender and the tough. The same Jesus who gripped that scourge of cords and drove the moneychangers out of the temple swept little children up into his arms.

If anyone gives you even a cup of water because you belong to the Messiah, I tell you the truth, that person will surely be rewarded.　　　　Mark 9:41 NLT

And without faith it is impossible to please God, because anyone who comes to him must believe that he exists and that he rewards those who earnestly seek him.　　　　Hebrews 11:6 NIV

REWARD AND PUNISHMENT MUST BE BALANCED.

When children are punished in public and embarrassed, they will resent it. Resentment, not removed by repentance and prayer, can degenerate into rebellion. Too many times recognition is shown only for bad behavior. That only reinforces it.

Punishment is hard on everyone. Rewards work wonders.

Hope deferred makes the heart sick; but when dreams come true at last, there is life and joy.   Proverbs 13:12 TLB

REWARD IN PUBLIC — PUNISH IN PRIVATE.

A father is only qualified to lead his family to the degree he is willing to serve them. Leaders can never stop serving, for when they do, they will no longer be qualified to lead. Knowing when to be led and when to lead is the wisdom of a real leader. Serving is not servitude. Serving is voluntary—servitude is involuntary. Leading is serving. Serving is ministry. Learn to minister. Serve capably and well. Work for the benefit of others. Even Christ took a towel and washed his disciples' feet.

Son of man came not to be ministered unto, but to minister.
Matthew 20:26-28 KJV

He that is greatest among you, let him be as the younger; and he that is chief, as he that doth serve.
Luke 22:26 KJV

Your care for others is the measure of your greatness.
Luke 9:48 TLB

YOU DON'T PUSH STRING, YOU PULL IT. YOU DON'T PUSH PEOPLE, YOU LEAD THEM.

We are shaped by the books we read and the friends we keep. Be aware of what your child is reading, listening to, and watching.

Peer pressure occurs throughout a lifetime. Be deliberate about putting your child in settings of positive peers. Positive peers will help guard their hearts from the influence of the culture. Positive peers can often be found at church. Churches provide powerful spiritual health benefits for them and you. Children must be taken to church and must see their father engaged in church.

Do not be partakers with them. For you were once darkness, but now *you are* light in the Lord. Walk as children of light.
Ephesians 5:7-8. NKJV

SIN IS CONTAGIOUS; RIGHTEOUSNESS IS NOT.

Repentance is not an apology for mistakes but a genuine desire to admit sin, forsake the wrong, and turn to embrace the right. Repentance is a command, not an option.

Now I rejoice, not that you were made sorry, but that your sorrow led to repentance... For godly sorrow produces repentance *leading* to salvation, not to be regretted; but the sorrow of the world produces death.

2 Corinthians 7:9-10 NKJV

HUMAN SORROW IS SORROW FOR GETTING CAUGHT. GODLY SORROW IS SORROW FOR WHAT CAUSES WRONG.

Jesus was a gentle man, but he was not a soft man. He said if your hand offends you, cut it off. He meant that when you are tempted to do what is not right, have the ruthlessness and self-discipline to get away from it. We must learn to be ruthless with ourselves at times. But, we are gentle with others. Gentleness is a sign of true strength in a man, not weakness. Insecure men compensate for their lack by abusing others. When a man knows his strength, he can afford to be gentle.

Your gentleness has made me great.
Psalm 18:35 NKJV

Be ye kind one to another, tenderhearted, forgiving one another.
Ephesians 4:32 KJV

BE RUTHLESS WITH SELF, GENTLE WITH OTHERS.

Adam sinned in Eden and, as a result, hid from God. Guilt, fear, and hiding, the sequentially ordered result of sin, is still the same today. Guilt weighs heavily and leads to fear. So, people hide. They try to escape. Escape reality. Escape responsibility. But—getting rid of guilt by any method other than repentance just makes you right in your own eyes— it's self-justification, buck passing. Every father must answer for his own actions. And—he answers to God alone. Repentance is the only means by which guilt can be released. For fathers, for children.

They heard the sound of the LORD God walking in the garden in the cool of the day, and Adam and his wife hid themselves from the presence of the LORD God among the trees of the garden… [Adam] said, "I heard Your voice in the garden, and I was afraid because I was naked; and I hid myself."

Genesis 3:8-10 NKJV

THE SEQUENTIALLY ORDERED RESULT OF SIN IS GUILT, FEAR, AND HIDING.

Farmers know the pattern of the harvest is: Condition the soil, sow the seed, water it, reap the harvest. Reaping the harvest is the last step, the goal. For fathers, the pattern of the harvest will always work to your benefit, if you'll start by conditioning the soil.

"You cannot mold clay when it is dry," simply points to the first step. Condition the soil of your child's heart to hear. When the child is ready to receive the seed, give the lesson. Water and encourage that seed, then reap the desired result.

To everything *there is* a season, A time for every purpose under heaven.

Ecclesiastes 3:1 NKJV

O Lord, you are our Father. We are the clay, and you are the potter. We all are formed by your hand.   Isaiah 64:8 NLT

YOU CANNOT MOLD CLAY WHEN IT IS DRY.

In the home, you represent the king and your family is the kingdom. When your character is negative, so are the characteristics of those in the home. To punish your children for what you see wrong in their lives is an error if it is also a characteristic of your life. Discipline yourself first, then others. You cannot correct in others what is wrong in your own life.

Train up a child in the way he should go: and when he is old, he will not depart from it.   Proverbs 22:6 KJV

FATHERS WHO PUNISH CHILDREN FOR DOING WRONG WHEN THEY HAVEN'T FIRST TAUGHT THEM HOW TO DO RIGHT, ARE THEMSELVES WRONG.

What you believe is the basis for conduct, character, and destiny. To change conduct, change beliefs. If you believe you're going to be poor, you'll overspend. If you believe you're dumb, you'll under-study. If you believe you're going to be killed, you'll avoid going out. If you believe people won't like you, you'll stop meeting people.

However, if you believe you're going to be healthy, you'll eat right. If you believe you're going to succeed, you'll look for opportunities. If you believe you're going to be rich, you'll invest. If you believe you can achieve your dreams, you'll pursue them.

Don't copy the behavior and customs of this world, but let God transform you into a new person by changing the way you think. Then you will learn to know God's will for you, which is good and pleasing and perfect.   Romans 12:2 NLT

ALL WRONG CONDUCT IS BASED ON WRONG BELIEVING.

The sin of omission is the basic sin of humanity. Husbands don't get in trouble when they fix the screen door, or fix the leaky faucet, but when they don't do it.

If we made all the right decisions and did all the right things every moment of the day, we'd never do anything wrong. But, by failing to fill our minds with godly thoughts and divine truths, failing to meditate on that which is true, a thousand fragments of filth will swarm in.

Every man must fight the sin of omission. He must minister to his family, know what their needs are, and help meet them.

To him who knows to do good and does not do *it*, to him it is sin.

James 4:17 NKJV

THE ONLY REASON YOU DO WRONG IS BECAUSE YOU DON'T DO RIGHT.

Love provides the basis for speaking the truth. And truth will set free.

But speaking the truth in love, [in all things—both our speech and our lives expressing His truth], let us grow up in all *things*.   Ephesians 4:15 AMP

And you shall know the truth, and the truth shall make you free.

John 8:32 NKJV

THE TRUTH MUST BE SPOKEN WITH LOVE.

PAVING YOUR
CHILD'S FUTURE

Some men are more mature at seventeen than others are at forty-seven. As long as a man is in denial, refusing to accept responsibility for his own actions, he cannot find help for his problems. Neither can he be responsible for success until he is willing to accept responsibility for failure.

David was the youngest. Now the three oldest followed Saul. David said to Saul, "Let no man's courage fail because of him (Goliath). Your servant will go out and fight with this Philistine."

1 Samuel 17:14, 32 AMP

MATURITY DOESN'T COME WITH AGE BUT BEGINS WITH THE ACCEPTANCE OF RESPONSIBILITY.

Feelings follow actions. To change your feelings, change your actions. Acting before you think is a sign of immaturity. Thinking before you act is a sign of maturity.

Much of our world is in the grip of a new psychology that says that feeling is more important than thinking. The words "I feel" are replacing "I think" even in government. But millions of people have lost everything because they acted in one foolish moment before they stopped to think.

Mature men put away childish things. They think before they act.

When I was a child, I spoke as a child, I understood as a child, I thought as a child; but when I became a man, I put away childish things.

1 Corinthians 13:11 NKJV

CHILDREN FEEL, ACT AND THEN THINK. MEN FEEL, THINK AND THEN ACT. LEADERS THINK, ACT AND THEN FEEL.

A man's inconsistencies are usually testimonies to his immaturity. There is a vast difference between being childlike and childish. Youth has its virtue, old age has its glory, but just acting like a child all your life is another matter. Irresponsibility, foolishness, and insensitivity are blemishes on a person's character. To accept responsibility, make wise decisions, and serve others are the signs of maturity.

Let this mind be in you which was also in Christ Jesus.   Philippians 2:5 NKJV

YOU'RE ONLY YOUNG ONCE, BUT YOU CAN LIVE IMMATURE FOR A LIFETIME.

How you handle change shows your level of maturity. People who refuse to change can't grow — physically, mentally, emotionally, morally, or in your family. Without growth there is no maturing.

Your attitudes and thoughts must all be constantly changing for the better.

Ephesians 4:23 TLB

But we all, with open face beholding as in a glass the glory of the Lord, are changed into the same image from glory to glory.

2 Corinthians 3:18 KJV

THE ONLY CONSTANT IN MATURITY IS CHANGE.

Two-thirds of our lifetime impressions are made before we are seven years old, we are told. Most of life's basic knowledge, such as the ability to read and write, is given to us before we are ten years old. This is why American educators can give college aptitude tests before students are thirteen years of age.

What happens to us in our early years creates images and causes us anxiety, stress, and tension later in life. It's true in all of us. Every image created has the potential for good or harm.

For as he thinks in his heart, so *is* he.

Proverbs 23:7 NKJV

WE ARE MOTIVATED TO BECOME WHAT WE IMAGINE OURSELVES TO BE.

Resisting the extraneous, illegitimate, and unnecessary allows for occupation with the productive, positive, and vital. Saying "yes" to the right gives the ability to say "no" to the wrong.

━━━━━━━━━━━━━━━━━━━━━━━

To everyone who conquers and continues to do my works to the end, I will give authority over the nations.

Revelation 2:26 NRSV

SUCCESS IS NOT BASED ON THE ABILITY TO SAY "YES" BUT ON THE ABILITY TO SAY "NO."

The simple reason for the work ethic is the dignity of man. When God gave manna in the wilderness, he could have given it a month at a time. Instead, he gave it on a daily basis so work was provided and dignity was given. Without working for what he is eating, a man is living off someone else's dignity.

If anyone is not willing to work, then he is not to eat, either.

2 Thessalonians 3:10 AMP

Work hard so God can say to you, "Well done." Be a good workman, one who does not need to be ashamed when God examines your work.   2 Timothy 2:15 TLB

THE WORK ETHIC BEGINS IN CHILDHOOD TO MAKE READY FOR THE WORK FORCE— WITHOUT A WORK ETHIC, NO FORCE IN WORK.

Fathers have long striven to give their children "a better life than I had." They establish trusts and college funds; they pull strings behind the scenes to get jobs for their children; they pave the way however they can. But material things, in the long run, may mean little. Nothing substitutes for real fathering.

The child needs a father, not a guardian angel. The child comes equipped with a guardian angel as a standard feature. To have a real father should also be a standard feature, not a luxury option.

Those who trust in their wealth and boast in the multitude of their riches, none *of them* can by any means redeem *his* brother, nor give to God a ransom for him. Psalms 49:6-7 NKJV

A TRUST FUND IS NO SUBSTITUTE FOR A FUND OF TRUST.

Each of us has weaknesses and strengths. Success comes by working through our strengths, not by dwelling on our weaknesses. We don't ignore our weaknesses, but being successful in our strengths makes our weaknesses less visible. If all you do is work on your weaknesses, you will lift them to average, and lower your strengths to the same level.

If a great guitarist worked on his weak jump shot every day and neglected his guitar—eventually he'd be an out of work guitarist and a mediocre basketball player.

God has given each of us the ability to do certain things well.   Romans 12:6 TLB

YOU DON'T MAKE A SUCCESS IN LIFE BY CONCENTRATING ON YOUR WEAKNESSES BUT BY GOING TO YOUR STRENGTHS.

To do something once is skill, but to do it habitually is the result of practice. Practice does not make perfect—it makes for excellence. Perfection is impossible— excellence is possible.

Practice doesn't create excellence, practicing properly does. Improper practice, no matter how diligently pursued, will produce imperfect skills. To be excellent is achieved by practicing the authentic skill.

Real men know that excellence in life is best achieved by practicing truth—and that comes from being led by the Spirit of God.

Let your light shine before men in such a way that they may see your good deeds *and* moral excellence. Matthew 5:16 AMP

EXCELLENCE IS NOT THE ABILITY TO DO SOMETHING ONCE, BUT TO DO IT SUCCESSIVELY SUCCESSFULLY.

Teach your children to act with courage in the classroom, on the campus, at home. Not to wait until their youth is gone to get the guts or wisdom to make their lives count. Do it now! Teach them not to allow themselves to develop bad thought patterns and habits that they'll have to undo and relearn later in life. Help them lay the right foundation to their character. Teach them to have the courage to begin right now, so they won't have to suffer all the remorse, regret, and retribution later.

Don't let anyone look down on you because you are young, but set an example. 1 Timothy 4:12 NIV

YOU'RE NEVER TOO OLD AND NEVER TOO YOUNG TO LEARN. YOU'RE NEVER TOO YOUNG AND NEVER TOO OLD TO BE USED BY GOD.

MAJORING IN MEN®
CURRICULUM

MANHOOD GROWTH PLAN

Order the corresponding workbook for each book, and study the first four Majoring in Men® Curriculum books in this order:

MAXIMIZED MANHOOD: Realize your need for God in every area of your life and start mending relationships with Christ and your family.

COURAGE: Make peace with your past, learn the power of forgiveness and the value of character. Let yourself be challenged to speak up for Christ to other men.

COMMUNICATION, SEX AND MONEY: Increase your ability to communicate, place the right values on sex and money in relationships, and greatly improve relationships, whether married or single.

STRONG MEN IN TOUGH TIMES: Reframe trials, battles and discouragement in light of Scripture and gain solid footing for business, career, and relational choices in the future.

Choose five of the following books to study next. When you have completed nine books, if you are not in men's group, you can find a Majoring in Men® group near you and become "commissioned" to minister to other men.

DARING: Overcome fear to live a life of daring ambition for Godly pursuits.

SEXUAL INTEGRITY: Recognize the sacredness of the sexual union, overcome mistakes and blunders and commit to righteousness in your sexuality.

THE UNIQUE WOMAN: Discover what makes a woman tick, from adolescence through maturity, to be able to minister to a spouse's uniqueness at any age.

NEVER QUIT: Take the ten steps for entering or leaving any situation, job, relationship or crisis in life.

REAL MAN: Discover the deepest meaning of Christlikeness and learn to exercise good character in times of stress, success or failure.

POWER OF POTENTIAL: Start making solid business and career choices based on Biblical principles while building core character that affects your entire life.

ABSOLUTE ANSWERS: Adopt practical habits and pursue Biblical solutions to overcome "prodigal problems" and secret sins that hinder both success and satisfaction with life.

TREASURE: Practice Biblical solutions and principles on the job to find treasures such as the satisfaction of exercising integrity and a job well done.

IRRESISTIBLE HUSBAND: Avoid common mistakes that sabotage a relationship and learn simple solutions and good habits to build a marriage that will consistently increase in intensity for decades.

JUST A BARTENDER: A captivating story of endurance and victory against overwhelming obstacles. The discovery of a man's identity against the backdrop of slavery, negative forces, and a world in turmoil. Stories that every man will identify with—to discover a new source of strength for himself.

ABOUT THE AUTHOR

Dr. Edwin Louis Cole (1922–2002), known as "the father of the Christian men's movement," was called by God to speak with a prophetic voice to the men of this generation. To that end, he founded the Christian Men's Network, a ministry that majors in men and communicates the reality that manhood and Christlikeness are synonymous.

A former pastor, evangelist, missionary, business executive, and denominational leader, Dr. Cole and his wife, Nancy, served the Lord together for more than fifty years. Over four million copies of his books are in circulation in more than forty languages, including his best-selling *Maximized Manhood*. Since his death, his legacy and vision have been carried on by his "sons" in the faith as they reach tens of thousands of men each month via books, videos, and other media.

Read more about the movement he started at CMN.men